Windows 10 for Beginner's

(A Beginners guide to Windows 10 with virtual illustrations)

BONIFACE BENEDICT

DEDICATION

This book is dedicated to God Almighty for his loving-kindness upon me.

Table of contents

Acknowledgment

I acknowledge my friends and well-wishers, especially Kane, Kingsley, and Stella, for their support during my days in school.

Introduction

This book is a guide strictly meant for those who are yet or have just started using the Windows 10 OS. This will guide them on how to master the functions and get used to the new layouts and displays the Windows 10 has to offer. Also, it will show you how to properly use Windows 10 OS right from when you power on your PC to when you put it off after operation.

It is no doubt that Windows 10 is way different in outlook and operation from other OS. It is why many users find the OS challenging to operate- usually in their first contact; however, with this book, you will find everything you need to get yourself acquainted to the OS.

Furthermore, included in the book are some of the common problems new users complain about, and interestingly, possible solutions to these problems. Read through every line of this book and move from being a Windows 10 OS Dummy to being a Master.

Chapter One

What is windows 10?

Chances are very high that you have heard and read so much about the Windows OS- mainly Windows 10. In fact, a lot of people across the globe are puzzling and trying their way through with the Windows 10 OS due to its complexity in layouts and user interface. The good news is that your searching and seeking will end as you are about to learn about the new upgrade. With this chapter, you will learn about the basics of windows 10 and why it is installed on your computer. Also, you will realize how it differs from older OS- this will get you into your first love with the upgrade.

What is Windows 10?

Windows 10 is software sold and created by a company called Microsoft. One differentiating fact about Windows OS is that it is not like the usual software that allows you to make income taxes calculation and send a bunch of angry emails to whosoever you wish to- Windows is more than that. Windows is an operating system which means that it controls every function you perform on your PC and it has remained that way for about three decades, Windows 10 is just a recent upgrade.

The name Windows came to existence as a result of all the little Windows the OS places on your computer screen, all having diverse functions. These Windows display different information like a baffling program, pictures as well as documents and files. You can decide to run these programs simultaneously while you jump from one window to the other and visiting one program and the other with less stress. You can also choose to make all your works based on one window, which fills the entire screen.

Now, know that every computer sold from July 2015 has the Windows 10 OS preinstalled in it; this means that you cannot escape the hurdles of this program except you will be opting for an apple PC- those beautiful looking PCs that cost more and leaves you to your isolated world.

The Start Menu

Firstly, the good news is that the new Windows 10 upgrade comes with the Start menu- that sounds very good. However, the bad news is that the Start menu is very different from older versions of the Windows OS. Although unusual, the Start menu is still somewhat identical to older versions; just a click on the Start button pops up all programs and applications on your PC. The significant difference is in the layouts and interface, which could be somewhat confusing,

4

it only gets easy for tablet owners who can get on the large tiles of applications with just a tap of their fingertip.

In that regard, through this chapter, you will learn how to navigate through the Start button, either you are running the OS from your PC, tablet, or desktop.

For desktop and PC owners, click on the start button at the lower left-hand side of your computer. Instantly, the start menu comes up, which displays large and small tiles of all available programs and applications on your computer. Click on whichever program you want to use and get started.

For tablet owners using the Windows 10 OS, the start button is located in the same position as it is for PC and desktops. Click on the Start button at the lower left-hand side of your tablet, this action displays the Start menu, then, with your fingertip, tap on any program you want to use. You can as well make the process faster by using the search menu to look for the program you wish to launch.

The reason for the difficulty in the Windows 10 OS is because it is designed to work on PCs, desktop, and tablets. Also, on older versions of Windows OS, the Start menu only covers a little- not even up to half- of your computer screen while on Windows 10, it covers the whole of your computer screen, leaving no space uncovered.

Adding to the fact that Windows 10 looks different, the OS still allows users to adjust Windows settings, start programs, find help for some tough situations and thankfully, shut down your computer.

On the Windows 10 OS, you can also customize the Start menu, remove apps and programs you do not need, and replace them with the most needed ones. You can as well place your most-used apps side by side. It gets as easy as the Start menu has two columns- one for the name of the app while the other is for tiles.

Take a chance by organizing the apps and programs to give you some comfort when visiting the page.

How can you do this?

To remove a tile, you do not need, Right-click on any program, and click on unpin from start menu- do this for all apps and tiles you do not need.

If you want to move a tile close to each other, hold the tile and drag to your desired position.

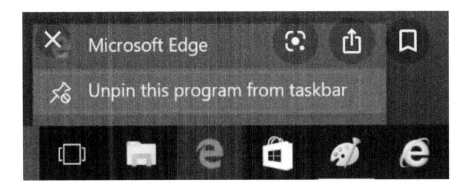

To add a new tile to your start menu, right-click from the start menu, a vertical bar of options appears, click on the new tile. Name the tile whichever way you want and add your desired apps and programs therein.

The Traditional Desktop

On Windows 10 OS, there is no significant difference with older versions; users can still perform diverse functions simultaneously on the desktop. The desktop also retains its three main parts- The Start button, Taskbar, and the Recycle bin. All icons on the desktop remain visible and accessible unless you make changes to them.

Basic Windows 10 Mechanics

One thing the Windows 10 start menu boasts of is bright colors, large buttons, and big letters, which makes it easy for you to see what you are selecting- or about to select- while also making navigations on the start menu easy.

By contrast, the OS includes many borders and features that might make it somewhat cumbersome to check through the start menu, however, the information mentioned above on the start menu is believed to help you move through the basic functions of the Windows 10.

Chapter Two
How programs, apps, and files function on Windows 10

When using Windows, it is important to note that applications and programs are your basic tools. Documents, on the other hand, are what you create using the installed programs and applications on your PC. This chapter better explains beyond the basics of opening a program and using an application; it shines a brighter light on how to launch a program, find it from the start menu as well as how they function on your system.

Starting an application or program

Windows 10 does not put the start menu and button in a tough to locate position as it retains the old corner spot as older Windows. As explained earlier, a click on the start button pops up the new look of the start menu, which is designed in a way that hangs a band of applications and programs present on your PC.

On this start menu, you will find a lot- not all- of the applications and programs present on your computer; from these displayed programs you can launch anyone you wish to use at the moment. Contrarily, if your desired application is not displayed, you can as well search through the search button to locate your program.

Among the functions that could be performed on the start, the menu includes arranging, deleting, and adding tiles and folders. This action helps organize your files and documents and put the most used in the best places to aid your search and use when next you search or visit the page.

Another way to start a program or application is by double-clicking on the icon on the desktop. Aside from arranging tiles and folders on the start menu, another way to make it easy for you to navigate through your programs is by adding them as an icon on the desktop. This way, you get to launch your program just by double-clicking on it just as it is with older Windows OS.

Playing with documents, programs, and files.

When properly seasoned, you will find out that you play with documents whenever you launch an application or package, for example, Microsoft Word- where you open a new document, save, edit and delete files. Windows OS is a big fan of standardization, which is why they allow users on diverse Windows OS to load their documents in very similar ways. When and how do you play with a document? You play with a document when you;

Open a Document

Documents and files are those things you create using an application or program- which is why the latter subheading was about launching a program. Now that you can start a program, how do you use the application or program to open and edit a document?

There are three known ways to open a document. These ways are just the same as when you perform the same action on older Windows OS; the only significant difference is the layouts.

- To get started, click on the word file which is located on the program's menu bar

- When the file menu pops up, click on open
- Finally, when all the files are displayed, select whichever one you wish to open. The program also goes in accordance with your command and subsequently opens the file and displays it on your screen.

Save a document

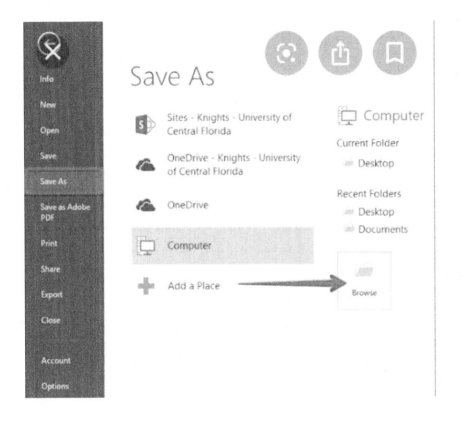

Basically, saving a file or document means restoring all changes made in the file and safekeeping it for further usage. Unless you specifically command your computer to perform this action, it will never save your files for you as it assumes that you have just been playing around for all the hours you have spent on it. Hence, giving out the command is essential, thanks to Microsoft for making this action less cumbersome on all their upgrades. With knowledge in windows 7, you can save your files on Windows 10 as well- just a little upgrade.

How do you save a document?

- The most used method is by clicking a file on the top menu, then select SAVE to save your document on your PC for retrieval and easy access next time.
- Another way to save files and documents is either by using the "CTRL+S" command; this automatically saves your file. Or by clicking on the save icon displayed in the margin.

It is noteworthy that when saving a file for the first time, Windows will request of you a name with which to save it on your PC. You are expected to type a kind of descriptive name using letters, spaces, and numbers that allow you to access the file easily.

Uninstalling Applications and Programs

Did you download an application or program that now seems to be troubling you? Or do you wish to free up some space on your PC by uninstalling some less frequently used applications? This action is very easy and is almost the same as when performing the same action on older windows OS.

To uninstall an application from your PC right from the start menu

- Right-click the application's tile on the start menu.
- Subsequently, this pops up a number of actions, click on uninstall and watch the application get rid of itself from your PC.

Locating missing files and programs

In this section, you will find how to locate missing files, applications, and programs on your PC. This function on the Windows 10 OS is solely found in the windows search box located next to the start button where you can access the start menu. The series of steps in the subsequent lines better explains how you can get this done.

- Type in whatever you are looking for in the search box

As said earlier, the windows search box allows you to find any file, program, or application on your system. You can access this through the start menu by typing it in; you will notice that as you begin typing it in, Windows immediately search for matches and display that to you simultaneously.

- Find with Cortana

Windows 10 is a very user-friendly and easy to use OS, some of the features that testify to this is Cortana- a personal digital assistant. Windows built Cortana in a way that it simplifies the OS by performing beyond finding missing files; the digital assistant also gives helpful information about you as well as your surroundings like traffic information and weather updates.

Cortana can be further explained to be the brain behind your search box as it also carefully listens through the microphone and awaits when you spill out the phrase "Hey Cortana" and subsequent words from you for it to help you find some hidden files and programs.

In this chapter, it is believed that you have learned beyond the basics of operating and running a program, file cum application; hence, you can easily and properly play with

16

files and programs as well as find them when they seem tricky to locate.

Chapter Three
Using the internet

Once you start using Windows 10, it automatically seeks updates and connections to the internet. Know that Windows 10 is way different from any other OS you have been running in previous times, this is why you are seeking ways to master the operations of the new upgrade. Undoubtedly, it must have cost Microsoft a couple of years to put this new OS together, and now that you have it, you must use it wisely.

Understanding how to use the internet on the Windows 10 OS is very important, adding to the fact that the OS automatically make updates to make the OS run smoothly. Windows also make these updates and checking to be sure you are not installing a pirated copy of the OS.

The Windows 10 OS is very web-dependent, and this is why it comes built with Microsoft Edge. Interestingly, Microsoft edge is very sleek and fast while helping you access and utilize the internet to your biggest advantage. Microsoft

Edge is a universal and well-reputed browser; this means it works well and in similar ways, whether being used on Windows 10 PC, tablet or phone.

In this chapter, the modus operandi of Microsoft Edge is well explained. Also, there is an exposition on how to connect with the internet, search, and visit websites as well as locate what you are seeking online.

Using the Internet

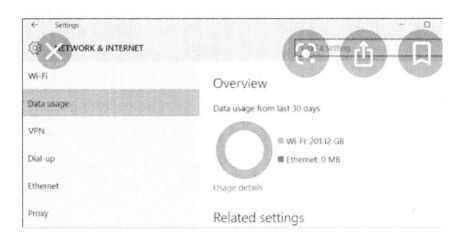

To connect with the internet and check in to any website you wish to, you need three basic things, namely: a PC, a web browser, and an internet service provider- these three things will give you uninterrupted access to the internet.

Now, it is certain that you already have the device- PC, tablet, or phone- while Microsoft Edge; the native browser on your PC handles the web browser part. This leaves just one of the three things you need to be left out, and that is your internet service provider, which is the major link to the internet.

A lot of times, when you try connecting to the internet, and it seems like Windows are not creating your access to the internet, it means there is a fault or error in connection rising from your internet service provider. People walk into restaurants, coffees, and other places where they can find a wireless connection; however, connecting with ISPs usually cost you some money. It is also important to know which ISP functions well and offers the best services in your geographical location. This is to avoid being stuck to a poor or bad ISP- it will cost you a stable internet connection.

How do you connect wirelessly to the internet?

Windows has always searched for internet connection whenever your system scans the airwaves for a Wi-Fi connection or your PC plugs into a cable. This helps Windows to easily connect with any previous Wi-Fi connection available at the moment; this connection is then passed on to Microsoft Edge. The next lines explain better how you can connect to the internet wirelessly.

- Once again, the start menu has another part to play in connecting you to the internet- although less role. Click on the start menu to get started.
- This pops up all programs on your PC, click settings.
- After clicking on settings, the internet icon, and settings application network displays, this opens to show you the available networks you can connect to. If your PC, tablet, or Smartphone can connect wirelessly, you gain access to connect to any of the listed available networks.
- Choose your desired connection by clicking on the name and subsequently clicking on connect. When connecting to an unsecured connection- networks that require no password for connection- you get connected automatically by clicking on connect. For a secured connection, you will need to enter the password to get connected to the network.
- Once the latter is successful, you can enjoy uninterrupted access to the internet.

In some cases, after trying all the connections available, Windows still does not connect you to the internet, it then offers you the Network Troubleshooter which scans your problem and gives a response about your connection. Disregard whatever response or solution the Troubleshooter suggests, what it is really saying is for you to get closer to the wireless transmitter.

Using the internet with Microsoft Edge

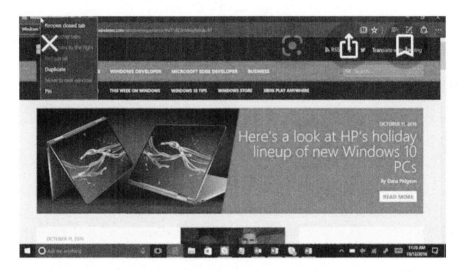

Microsoft Edge is built for speedy and hasty connection to the website; this is made obvious in the rate at which it loads and displays web pages- however, in accordance with the speed permitted by your ISP. In addition to its speed also lies its limitation; in a bid to speed up connection and show every content of the website, Microsoft Edge hides its menu bar.

To get started with Microsoft Edge, click on the program icon, which is located on the taskbar somewhere on the bottom of your screen once you click on this icon, the application opens which either open as your last visited site or a new screen that displays weather, top news as well as links to popular and well-known sites.

Although, this new browser from Microsoft hides all its menus behind cryptic icons virtually, however, you can still easily locate the ones mentioned in subsequent lines.

- Back: This is located on the top left corner. Its basic function is to allow you to revisit your last visited page
- Forward: This is located just beside the back button. It lets you check back to a page you just left.
- Refresh: This becomes very useful when visiting news sites; it allows you to reload the site and get the most recent update from the page. It is located just beside the right arrow-forward.

- Tabs: Both the site you are working on and your previously visited sites are accessible once they are opened as tabs. It is situated along the Windows top edge-very close to the refresh key.

Other menus that are hidden on the Microsoft Edge browser include open new tab, address bar, add to favorite or reading list, reading view, web note, hub, share, and more. Even with the new outlook of the browser, all these menus that seem to be hidden can easily be located on the top screen of Microsoft edge.

Socializing on Windows 10: mail, calendar and more

The internet has already become a very important tool in socializing and meeting new people as well as getting back on old friends. It is no news that the internet has connected and linked up a lot of people daily; Microsoft is not leaving you alone to your world either.

In a bid to offer the best services to users, Microsoft has included some new functions in the Windows 10 OS to enhance your social life. These features are mail, calendar, and people-you can easily guess which application handles a particular function as the name suggests.

A lot of the features in the windows 10 OS are things you have previously accessed on older OS; a little upgrade made it complicated. More importantly, if you have used the People on older OS, then you might need to take some time to understand that the new application on Windows 10 does not integrate your social accounts. When viewing a friend's account, it only displays their basic information and not their Facebook or Twitter as in older times.

Unlike older OS, the Mail app on Windows 10 is built-in; this allows it to take control of receiving and sending messages on your PC. The application also updates you whenever a message comes in displaying the name of the sender as well as the body of the mail. The Windows 10 OS also brings the mail app supporting POP and IMAP accounts-this implies that the application works well on a wide range of email accounts.

Safe Computing measures

Just as every OS from Microsoft, Windows 10 is a very safe and highly secured end to end for every user. However, one can never decide safety when there are diverse users from diverse locations across the globe; due to the fact that they get opened to diverse applications, programs, files, and documents that could include viruses and other dangers that impede the perfect functioning of a computer. Here are some safeties measures that can help you retain your Windows 10 and keep it running as long as you desire.

- Do away with phishing scams
- Avoid viruses via Windows defender
- Use parental guides or children controls
- Never download applications or programs from unreliable sources
- When connecting to wireless connections-via WI-Fi-never connect to unsecured networks. These unsecured networks usually require no password to connect; hence, this leaves your PC prone to any kind of attack.

Chapter Four
Upgrading and Customizing Windows 10

One thing that can easily give pleasure to Windows 10 users is customizing the OS to look and appears the way you want it to. This practice is not new as it has always been present even in the older OS. However, you might be having slight difficulty in getting things done here- the interface is way different. Inorder To customize your Windows 10; there are two basic tools to perform this function;

- **Control Panel**

The control panel happens to be a well-known tool right from the very first Windows OS; it has been and still remains very handy for making adjustments on your Windows 10 OS.

- **Settings App**

The settings app is the most accessible way to customize Windows 10. The new changes in this app make it possess big and large buttons of which you may never need to leave the page- all you need to do is right present here.

Although, these two applications perform different settings, however, they still have similar functions and can also be found intertwined in one another. You can easily switch from the control panel to the settings app and vice versa.

How to change the appearance of your Windows

When it comes to changing the appearance of your Windows, you can do this under the Appearance and Personalization section of the Settings App. This function allows you to change the appearance, look, and behavior of your Windows 10 in a huge number of ways, as mentioned below.

- **Personalization**

The personalization settings allow you to decide your screen saver and some other petty touches that decide the way your system looks. In the new Windows 10 OS, most personalization settings now live in the settings apps; this way, you can navigate to an application's personalization settings with just a right-click on a blank part of your desktop- choose to personalize afterward.

- **Display**

While personalization allows you to touch your desktop and design it your way, display on the other hand- just as the name implies- allows you access your computer screen. With the display function, you get to control lettering, font size, screen resolution, and more.

- **File Explorer Option**

This part of the personalization and appearance settings is where you can manage and control how folders and files function on your PC. If you want to scale through the long hurdles of going through the appearance and personalization settings, open any folder, click on the View tab, then click on the options icon located on the right side.

Other functions that allow you to manage and control the appearance and behavior of your PC include Ease of Access Centre, Taskbar and Navigation cum Fonts. For some of these aforementioned, clicking on them takes you to a Control Panel setting where you can fully take charge of the controls. On the other hand, some take you to the right control in the settings app; but whichever way you still get to control and decide the look of your PC.

How to change the desktop background

Often referred to as wallpaper, the background is a picture on your desktop upon which all icons displayed on your PC rests on. It is somewhat certain that you might not like the image that comes with your Windows 10 OS; hence, you need to know how to replace it with your chosen picture. Learn this in the next few steps.

- Right-click on your desktop, some options display, choose to personalize.
- This action instantly kicks you to the settings application personalization page.
- Select a picture from the available background pictures. Microsoft has a number of already designed images that fit in as background images.
- If you do not like the images displayed for you, you can choose your own image.

- Click on the browse button below the page; subsequently, your picture folder pops up; from here, you can select your desired background image.
- Next is for you to decide the placement of your background image. This means whether you want to set it to fit, fill, tile, stretch, or make the image centered. All these actions are based on your image and also based on your choice of placements.
- After you have made your preferences, you are expected to save the changes by clicking on the SAVE button- without this, you have made no changes.

How to choose a screen saver

Questions about the difference between a screen saver and wallpaper will never stop arising. While both are about images displayed on your computer screen, they have different occasions which they apply. Wallpaper stays while your PC is on, the screen saver, on the other hand, are images that secedes the other while your computer is not in use. You can read through the subsequent lines to know how you can change it.

- Here, knowledge in start menu operation is essential. By clicking on the search box next to the start menu, search for a screen saver; subsequently, the screen saver settings Windows pop up.

- You will see an arrow pointing downward in the screen saver box, click on it, and select a screen saver from your library. After selecting the image or images, be sure to click on settings- this is because certain images will request of you the speed of a slide show and other specifications.

- You can also add security by selecting On Resume, Display Logon screen checkbox. This safeguards your computer from third party interference.

- Again, once your action is complete, click on OK to save all changes made.

How to change your computer's theme

Themes can be said to be a vast collection of settings that spice up your PC's appearance and outlook. This feature exists on all devices and OS; however, settings vary, and this is why you need to learn how to do this on your Windows 10 OS. Windows 10 offers you many themes; however, you can decide to save your favorite background and screen saver as your theme. This is how:

- **Windows Default Theme**

This category includes all the built themes from Windows, which include the original one- simply Windows.

- **My Themes**

Here, the themes you have personally created show here; also, if you have Microsoft account, you get to see a synchronized theme, i.e., the one you see on every PC.

- **Basic and High Contrast Themes**

This contains high contrast themes mostly for the visually impaired.

Chapter Five
Music, Movies and Photos functions

What makes a perfect OS and PC for some is the fun embedded in the device; aside from having a PC that works well as an office and home tool, there are times you need to have fun with your device. Tablet and cellphone owners of the Windows 10 OS can tell more about the need for fun on devices.

While older Windows allows you to have fun on your device with good games, music, videos, and photos, the absence of a traditional music application brought about the flaws therein, this upgrade is what Microsoft is introducing on the new Windows 10 OS with the new Windows 10 music app. This application sticks strictly to the basics and cores of its existence on the OS.

In this digital world of music and extensive fun, Microsoft also introduces the Microsoft Groove Music Pass. While this might require a monthly fee for it to be accessible, it remains very handy and useful as it allows you to navigate and check-in across any internet radio based on your own choice of the artist.

In this chapter, the exposition will be made on how music, photos, and videos function on the new Windows 10 OS as well as how to make navigations and utilize the upgrade to your greatest advantage.

Playing music with Microsoft Music App.

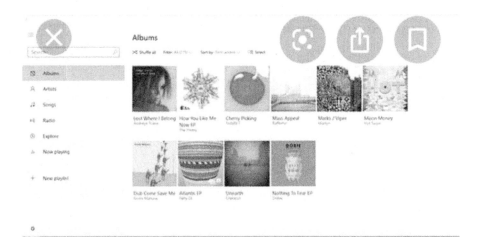

With this new upgrade, you definitely will want to explore and see what it is like to get on the new Microsoft music app- this is very important. Except if you run the OS on a tablet, you will want to do more than just playing your song and listening to it. Possibilities are high that you will want to organize your music based on categories, preferences, and artists- it gets easy with the Microsoft music app.

If you want to play music using the Microsoft music app, which gives a whole new experience, follow the steps below.

- Like the traditional way to launch a package on Microsoft, on the start menu, click the music tile. In contrast, if you cannot locate the music tile, click on all apps, this action brings all the applications and programs on your PC in alphabetical, choose the music app from this list.

- While the music app launches and fills your screen, you can start playing your music from here.

- To play music, click on an album title- or music- from the available music albums on your PC. Subsequently, the music app shows your song. Get the beats on by clicking on the play button.

- While the music app plays your song, you can make diverse adjustments like repeat, play, pause, shuffle, stop, next to or previous, and many others through icons displayed on the screen to help you control and decide how your music is played.

It is important to note that the music app continually plays your music even when you switch to another application or package. In a similar fashion, with the old Windows media player, you need to open the app back before you are able to pause between the song or change to another track.

Playing videos with the Microsoft music app
Now, many cellphones and digital cameras can capture good video of very high quality; hence, do not be astonished that videos now appear in Windows media player and the music app.

Playing a video with the music app is so much similar to playing music and songs within the same app; however, there exists a bit of difference. After following the same procedure in launching the application, click on videos in the navigation pane, which is located somewhere on the left-hand side. Subsequently, this action brings all the videos on your PC, and you are now left to choose whichever you want to launch- to open a video, double click on it.

Playing with photos

The other side of fun on Windows 10 OS aside from music and videos is photos; photos help you keep memories.

Hence, you have a million reasons to keep them safe. Adding to the fact that photos tell a very wide and long story, they have also helped maintain a level of recognition with the environment. While people are beginning to dump digital cameras to opt for their smartphones, Microsoft also gives you such convenience as they set up their new OS to make it easy for you to retain memories on your PC. The next lines show you how to save your Smartphone pictures on your PC using the Windows 10 OS.

Modern cellphones are beginning to possess inbuilt applications that allow it to easily connect with personal computers with little or no stress. That being said, you might not need to be bothered about your Smartphone not having such application, Microsoft has built software in the new upgrade that allows for an easy connection for cellphones and digital cameras- just as it is with the subsequent OS.

To get started;

- Plug your phone or camera into the computer using a cable. In most cases, digital cameras have two ports for cable- one for connection to television ready for viewing, and the other is for connecting to personal computers. You need to look for the right port and make the connection.

- Turn on your digital camera and unlock your cellphone, then, wait for file explorer to recognize it. In order to ease the recognition by explorer, open the file explorer. It is located along the taskbar on the bottom of your desktop. Once launched, you will find the connection of the cellphone or digital camera at the lowest part of the connected and available devices. Be sure your camera is in display mode before complaining that your device is not connecting.

- Finally, to move files, right-click on either of the cellphone or digital camera, and select import photos- this action gets the selected pictures moving to your personal computer.

These aforementioned actions are very similar in the mode of getting it done, what distinguishes Windows 10 from older OS is the interface and ease in launching new pages for action.

Chapter Six

Common problems of Windows 10

While everything that has a big advantage will always possess one or two bad sides, the new Microsoft Windows 10 is not left out in this category. Although the OS is very effective in operations, it is also prone to faults and ills.

There are times your system will just display an odd and unusual screen; then, what comes to your mind is that your PC is malfunctioning. When your system starts running slow, programs freeze, or the menu bar is not starting; now that it is building a fault.

In this chapter, you will know about some core and basic shortcomings, otherwise called problems, of the windows 10 OS as well as possible ways to get rid of them.

File and data lost

All systems and OS-including this windows 10 OS- is prone to virus attack, which impedes the normal functioning of the system. There are many ways in which an OS can come across viruses adding to the fact that they receive files and programs, some of which are from untrusted sources.

A virus attack on the system could be very hazardous that it often costs the user and owner of a PC a great loss. However, in case you fall victim to a virus attack, there are still ways t revive and restore your lost files. The latter is presented in subsequent lines.

• Firstly, for you to be able to restore lost files, you must have backed it up from file history- if you have performed the latter, proceed to the next lines.

• Open file explorer and perform a quick search on the item you have lost. If it does not pop up, try going through the source of the lost file or program- for example, documents or pictures.

• After finding the location, click on the home tab on top of the folder, and then choose history.

• Click on HISTORY by selecting history. You get to see all that has been backed up before it was lost.

• Next is for you to select the program you will like to have back- more explanation on that below.

Files- if you want to restore a file or group of files, just open the folder in which they are contained, so the files are fully shown on your screen.

Folder- to get back an entire folder; click on the folder after locating it so you can check through all its contents.

• Once you have located the file, you wish to retrieve, move forward and backward to view the different versions of the file.

• The different versions are made available upon the fact that these files are backed up on different dates, a more recent version of the file should be of higher priority as this is what defines the file to be more updated and covering what you need it for the most.

• After locating the file version, right-click on it and choose to restore the displayed options.

• Once you have selected this option, watch your file restore itself back to your PC. To avoid further issues of having your files lost, you can save the file in a very different location or rename it- based on your preferences.

• After completing this action, exit the file history and close the window.

Not enough space to install a Windows update
New updates are periodic and come in succession to the previous version; in this way, it usually consumes more space to install. To free up some space on your system, you are advised to install CleanMyPC. This helps to uninstall applications and related files that consume space; the application also takes out files that are still hanging around after you must have scanned your PC.

Another easy way to deal with this issue of not enough space for a Windows update is to use the built-in Disk Cleanup tool and follow the steps below.

1. Click on the Start menu
2. Choose All Programs
3. Select Accessories, then System Tools
4. Click on Disk Cleanup
5. Below the Files to delete heading, select which file types you want to remove

6. If you do not know which file type to delete, select them individually, read the description, and keep your desired ones.

PC boots slowly

There are many reasons why the Windows 10 OS might be booting slowly; one is if the present OS you are running is outdated, another reason could be due to malware. If you want to check if your system has been infected by malware, follow the steps below.

1. Press the Windows key alongside "I"
2. Select Update & Security
3. Choose Windows Defender
4. Click on Open Windows Defender
5. Press Full Scan and the scan now
6. Once the scanning is completed, follow the subsequent instructions displayed on your screen.

Files open in the wrong application.

Virtually every user opens a file by double-clicking on it; however, if the file association in Windows is already broken, the program will not launch in the right application as expected. To fix this;

1. Click on the Start menu
2. Choose settings
3. Click on the System tab and search for default apps
4. From the latter, you can decide what application opens each kind of file with specifications of apps for diverse file extensions

Windows uses 4G data when you don't want it to

Windows 10 and later versions of the Windows OS has auto-connected to background data. This might be hazardous when you get to know that downloads and background processes have been eating up your bandwidth without your consent. To correct this;

1. Click on the Start menu
2. Select Settings
3. Click Network & Internet
4. Select Wi-Fi, then Advanced Options

5. Change "Set as metered connection" to the ON position

You can't play DVD movies

An upgrade that might be of much concern to those who are very much into movies is the absence of a built-in DVD player. This might be due to the assumption from Microsoft that you watch your movies online; however, you can make a payment to Microsoft to enable you to download a DVD player. Also, you can download VLC; instead, it is free, works perfectly, and will play your DVDs.

Too many notifications

The Action Center in Windows 10 is a very commendable development for keeping all your notifications together. Contrarily, this can also piss users off when it becomes highly cluttered with messages that you have no interest in. Luckily, you can switch this off.

1. Go to the Start menu
2. Choose Settings
3. Click on System
4. Choose Notifications & Actions

5. You can use the toggle switches to control when and how notifications appear in that section- you can also set them to appear no more.

Your privacy settings aren't right for you

The default setting on Windows 10 seems not to be the best setting for everyone, as it allows for too much access to personal data from unauthorized parties. If you wish to make this more private, here is how to change it.

1. From the Start menu, go to Settings
2. Choose Privacy
3. Read through each section on the left-hand side in turn (Location, General, Microphone, camera, etc.)
4. Review the settings of each section and apply the toggle switches to make them suit your choice.

System Restore has gone missing

Debunk the rumor about the missing system restores on Windows 10, it has only turned off by default, of which the reasons are best known to Microsoft. You can bring this back to function by following the steps below.

1. Click on the Start menu

2. type 'system restore' into the search box

3. Select Create a restore point

4. When the System Properties panel shows, click on the System Protection tab

5. Make sure your C: drive is selected then press Configure

6. Afterward, Click the radio button next to Turn on system protection

7. Use the slider to specify how much of your hard drive to use for restore points — 5-10% should do it

Too many pop-ups in Edge

A bunch of ads can be very annoying and frustrating; however, Edge has a solution to this as it possesses a built-in pop-up blocker. To utilize this effect, use the steps below.

1. Click on the More button

2. Choose Settings

3. Proceed to View advanced settings.

4. Set Block pop-ups to "On."

Printer trouble

Printers could also be a form of trouble, due to the difference and newness in the interface and setup of Windows 10 OS, luckily, it can also be fixed with less stress.

1. Go to Control Panel
2. Choose Devices and Printers.
3. Right-click on your printer then choose to remove it.
4. Hence, go to your printer maker's website and download the latest drivers for your printer. After downloading it, follow the instructions to install them.

Broken Window

The case of a broken window could be more expensive than that of lost or misplaced files. While lost files can be restored, a broken window most likely has no way out of it upon the fact that a broken window implies that all your actions on the OS get totally restricted.

A broken could occur due to interference from an unauthorized third party- could be from a hacker- or due to a very high level of virus attack on the OS. In the case of a broken window, you might require the services of a computer engineer who will help restore your PC. Also, you can restore all your lost files through One Drive as well as via your Microsoft account- if you have created any before the data breach.

Strange messages

Strange messages and unusual information asking for permission are one of the quickest ways to detect and error in the proper functioning of Windows 10 OS. Just as older windows OS, this new upgrade also has two user accounts- administrator and the standard user accounts. While administrator account is meant for the owner of the PC and holds the major powers of running the system, on the other hand, standard accounts have restrictions to certain actions on the PC as it possesses certain features that can cause damage to the computer files and programs.

Whichever account you run, your system is still prone to popping up certain messages asking for permission. The latter is due to some attempts of changes that a program might be trying on the normal functioning of your PC. In most cases, when messages like this pop up, users and owners of the PC usually overlook the dangers posed therein and give their approval, even when it means their system is prone to a level of virus.

To avoid a huge risk and get your PC safe, whenever your system pops up the message in blue, ask yourself if you have made any action that warrants such a message or if the permission is needed in any way. If your answer to the latter is yes, then go ahead and allow the access, however, if otherwise, do not give your consent as this might cost you a huge loss from virus attack.

Moving from an old to a new Windows 10 PC

One of the most exciting moments for a PC owner is when you make the ultimate shift from an old window to windows 10 OS; this is often best done with a new PC. However, this joy could be cut off when you realize that you cannot get hold of your files on your old PC.

Before the advent of Windows 10 OS, there used to be an Easy Transfer application that allows for easy recovery, sending and receiving of applications and files. Sadly,

Microsoft discontinued this feature on Windows 10 OS, making it tedious to restore files from the old PC.

Now, if you want to upgrade to a new PC with Windows 10 OS

1. First, upgrade your old PC to windows 10
2. Create a Microsoft account- having a Microsoft account is not supported on older windows OS.
3. By creating a Microsoft account, you can then backup up your files and restore them on your new PC.

This way, you have solved one of the greatest problems faced by most users when moving from an old device to a new one.

Using the HELP on the windows help system
Complications are possible in the process of operating your windows 10 OS. This implies that there definitely a need for you to have helped on the OS. In the lines that follow, you will find the quickest and easiest ways in which windows give out help to users and owners of the device.

• Start menu- Microsoft gives help to you through the start menu; click on the Get Started tile and find some basic help.

• You can access help within any application or on the desktop by pressing F1.

• By going through settings, you can find help for basically anything you need by clicking on the HELP button.

• Also, if you spot any question mark on anywhere on your desktop or within an app, click on it, you will definitely find help.

How to stop automatic update on windows 10

To start automatic update in windows 10, you need to follow one of these two steps;

1. Go to "search" and type "service.msc or "service." It will bring the service app. Double click it to open it. It will open all the programs on the PC. Scroll down to windows update. Right-click on it. It will bring out "properties." Click on properties. It will bring you to the update page. Click on the drop-down on the "start-up" and change it from manual to "disable." Then click on "stop "besides the service type and

then click on apply and save. The update will automatically stop.

2. The second method is to upgrade your pc to the latest Windows 1909 version. It comes with a "pause update." Once you upgrade your PC. Click on setting – update – pause. You will be able to pause updates for 30 days.

Chapter Seven

Windows 10 tips for tablet and laptop owners

To any level of expertise and mastering of the operations and running of the Windows 10 OS, it is very certain that you will always- at some point- need help and some tips to help with some load of operations.

While the whole book itself is centered on helping you get yourself acquainted with the Windows 10 OS and master the modus operandi, this chapter has more focus on laptop and tablet owners of the new Windows upgrade, and how to help them carry out some simple and basic functions on it. It is more of "how-to."

Turning on Tablet mode

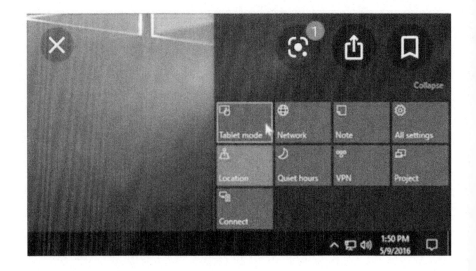

Tablet mode is a very desirable model on the Windows 10 OS due to some level of comfort that it gives to the user. When in tablet mode, your applications and program on the start menu fill the screen completely, upon the fact that tablets are a smaller version of desktop computers; hence, seeing one program at a time helps you centralize your focus on just one program.

To toggle the mode on your tablet;

- Slide in your fingers down from the right edge of your screen

- This action brings up the Action Centre pane.

- From the Action Centre pane, click the tablet mode button.

- This also pops up about four buttons from which you are to select from; they are: On/Off Toggle when I sign in when my device wants to Switch modes and Hide App icons on the taskbar when in Tablet mode.

How to switch to Airplane mode

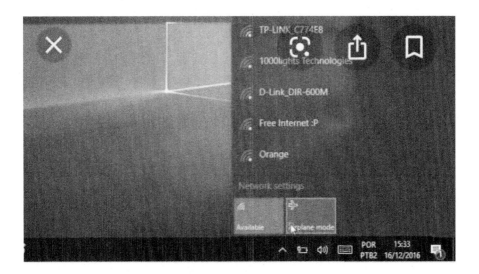

While traveling long distances and miles on an airplane, a lot of people keep themselves busy with games, movies and also performing some tasks that relate to their job- portable devices are best for this. However, a good number of airlines will require you to totally disconnect your wireless connections when the plane is in flight- this is called the airplane mode.

To avoid some sort of disgust for yourself when in this situation, learn how to easily switch to airplane mode in the next lines.

- Just as in the latter heading, open the Action Centre pane by sliding your finger into the screen from the screen's right edge.
- Next is to click or tap the word Expand on top of the row of buttons.
- As noted earlier, the action center pane usually displays four buttons on its bottom edge by tapping on Expand; you get to see some rows of hidden additional buttons.
- Finally, click or tap on the Airplane mode icon displayed on your screen. Subsequently, the button highlights, "Airplane Mode is turned on."

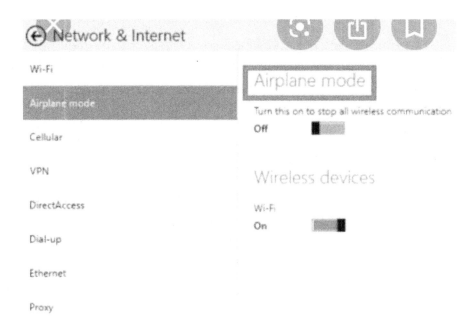

If you want to turn off airplane mode and get your system back to its latter state, repeat the same step reconnect to the internet, turn on your Bluetooth, radio, Wi-Fi, as well as GPS. Amazingly, flight mode is not only ideal for safety rules, but it also a better option for conserving your battery life.

How to connect to a wireless internet connection

Anytime you connect to a wireless connection, know that Windows save the settings for ease connection next time you visit. However, when connecting for the first time- as noted earlier- you can get your connection in the steps that follow.

- Turn on your PC wireless adapter- if your computer is in airplane mode, turn it off following the steps in previous instruction
- Click on the taskbar wireless network icon, which displays all the available wireless networks within its range.
- That been said, connect to a wireless network by clicking on its name and subsequently clicking on the connect button.

NB: when connecting to a network, it is not worthy that there are two types of network connection, i.e., Secured network and unsecured network. What distinguishes a secured network from an unsecured network is that the latter requires no password to get you connected to the network while the formal will as for password before you can have access to it. An unsecured network makes your system prone to data breach and unauthorized access/third party interference upon the fact that it requires no password for connection; hence the name unsecured. However, an unsecured network might be ideal when there is a poor connection, or you need to get something done very fast.

Toggling your tablet screen rotation

Windows 10 OS for tablets is usually held up horizontally, but if you pick on them, they automatically rotate to keeps your work vertical, making it long and narrow. In a swift response to that, Microsoft built this OS with auto-rotation, which is very useful when reading a digital book, which makes the long and thin pages look more real lie a printed boo.

Also, the auto-rotation feature is convenient when watching movies or showing some photos to your friends. The basic issue with auto rotation is when the screen rotates unexpectedly, causing some distraction on your PC; the good news is you can learn to loc auto rotation in the next few lines.

- Slide into the screen from the bottom right corner
- This launches the action center pane.

- Next is to tap or click the word expand above the four buttons; this reviews a number of actions and hidden buttons.
- Then click or tap the rotation lock button, which stops your screen from auto-rotating; you can as well unlock the autorotation to make it rotate.

How to adjust to different locations

You might never know the importance of being able to change your location and set it to diverse places until you travel out of your present location, and your time zone stuck you to your previous location. While you can still avoid this ill for yourself, it is best if you learn how to adjust your location now.

- Right from the desktop, right-click on the clock in the taskbar at the bottom right corner- a menu pops up this way.
- The settings app pop up to the time and language section
- Click on the adjust date and time.
- Afterward, click on the time zone option and choose your present time zone from the list of available options. This effect changes your time zone- which is an integral part that every traveler needs when in a new location.
- Make the preferred changes in your regions and languages as well as date and time for formats to match up with your present location. The settings application Time and language section also allow you to change speech, date, and time as well as region and language.
- After making all your desired changes, close the Settings app by clicking X in the top right corner.

How to backup your laptop before traveling

Backing up the files on your PC is very important, as this helps you feel your most cherished and handy files safe and able to access later when needed. While there are less traditional ways to backup files as introduced by older versions of the Windows 10 OS- this usually limits users to save their files on hard disks. However, hard disks are beginning to fail people as it poses some threats of crashing and leaving the user left with no bit of information.

Windows 10 came to the rescue as it allows users back their laptops automatically after purchase; only two things are required- stable internet connection and a Microsoft account. Also, users can have their files backed up on other platforms like One Drive and the likes. Undoubtedly, saving in the air is one of the best ways to back up your data and files as this is never going to crash, more so, you rest assured that there will be no sort of breach in your data upon the fact that it is well-secured end to end- unless you get careless with your passwords or allow third party access to your account.

How to access the mobility center

The mobility center introduced in Windows 7 still exists in Windows 10 OS as well, just that some upgrades have taken place. The mobility center is a collection of the most used and highly visited settings for all kinds of devices- portable and non-portable.

Accessing the mobility center comes with so much ease, to get started, right-click on the start button, and click on the mobility center from the options that pop up. Subsequently, the mobility center appears, leaving you to get on any operation as you so desire from this page.

PS: understand that diverse manufacturers and device makers have different ways of making users perform the same function, that being said, it implies that there are different settings varying from diverse makers. However, they all have similarities in rotation, quick ways to toggle around screen brightness as well as how to connect to projectors and monitors.

The latter stated, as well as other information passed across in this chapter, is to affirm and make exposition on the basis of Windows 10 tips for tablet and laptop owners. With these, it is expected and believed that on your next contact with your Windows 10 OS, you will perfectly- and with no stress- navigate through the functions of the operating system.

Chapter Eight
How to shut down the PC

De facto, you have learned how to start your computer and use it; and also how to perform diverse functions and use it for various tasks. After this, what is left? You should also know how to shut down your PC and make it take some break after long use. Right from the first versions of Windows OS, there have always been more than one or two ways to shut down your PC; however, in this chapter, you will be shown the two major and appropriate ways to shut down your PC. Know that, in no circumstance should you shut down your PC using the power button as this might affect the smooth functioning of your computer.

To turn off your PC, follow these steps.

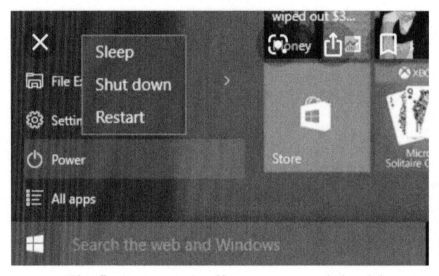

- The first way to turn off your computer is by right-clicking on the start button, which opens the Windows Menu.

- From this menu, a number of options are displayed at the lower part of the screen.

- Click on shut down or sign out; some four other options- sign out, sleep, shut down and restart- comes on the right, click on shut down to turn off the computer.

- Another way to shut down your PC is by clicking on the start button to launch the start menu. On the lower left-hand corner, you will find an option point to shut down the system, click on it and some three other options are displayed- shut down, restart and sleep- use shut down and watch your PC turn off.

- Aside from the ways listed above, there are some other tricky

- Ways to shut down your PC. Some of these ways are somewhat prone to damaging one or two things in your computer, while the others will just shut it down the usual way. Right from the older versions of the Windows OS, there is a short and fast way to tell your PC to take some rest. This requires just two commands, and that is by pressing ALT alongside F4 simultaneously; this shows a number of options- shut down, sleep, restart and hibernate. Choose shut down from these options, and the system turns off at the moment.

With the above, it is no doubt that you can shut down your PC in diverse ways based on your choice of preference.

Conclusion

Undoubtedly, Windows 10 is the most powerful and highly vast operating system amidst all other OS created by Windows. While this upgrade is the most powerful and highly handy

Of all, it remains highly complex in all forms, modes, and operations. The user interface introduced here is highly intuitive that it often requires new users to read well and understand all the components and units of the system- just as you are taking out time to read and understand the operations of the new OS.

In Windows 10, users will have to dig deep and deeper into the system before they can fully understand what it entails. Also, you will need to make a lot of customizations and changes on the OS to allow you to utilize what is embedded in it and maximized the experience to your utmost advantage. The aspects of the Edge browser, Cortana voice, and many other features require close attention due to the complexity of the programs; however, if adequately attended to, you will surely enjoy these features as they give more comfort and pleasure than the latter programs in previous programs. If you are still dwelling on Windows 7 or older OS or thinking of making the upgrade to a more recent Windows 10 OS, this piece has been put together for you to fully get you on track towards what is built in the OS cum your expectations.

At this point, it is no doubt that this book has fully filled your thirst in many ways; however, there are still some tips and facts to understand the Windows 10 OS. Know that there are no enough tips in the world to match up with what you need to get in track with the OS; there is really no tip like getting on the Windows yourself. As said in the former lines, these tips can only be known when you use the OS. That being said Just as it is with older versions of the Windows OS, some of the tips here are what you should meet up with as it is with keeping your system running, some of these tips are but not limited to;

- Never put off your system using the power button. As said in older chapters of this book, putting off your PC especially, with the power button, is a very wrong way to put off your system, unlike when you do this with the right way of shutting down your PC. The dangers posed by putting your PC off with then power button includes an instance that when your system is trying to shut down with the appropriate way, it signifies you if any application is running in the background and seeks the right way to quit the operation. Contrarily, using the power button does not show any information of such; it just goes off, leaving the background applications to get rid of themselves; this way, your PC gets prone to a lot of unexpected attacks like crashing of applications and programs when you least expected it to. This could be the reason why some of your applications do not function anymore, and you will have to install and reinstall over again.

- Another tip is that of Cortana virtual assistant. This virtual assistant helps you manage your schedule, gather important information, and also send messages whichever way you want it. The assistant also helps you reach out to applications and programs within your PC; sadly, the assistant will not give any aid unless you ask it to. How do you notify your Cortana of this help? Cortana is a virtual assistant that requires notification from your voice, just say "Hey Cortana," this gets your assistant in action.

There are many other tips as regards the proper running and functioning of the Windows 10 OS, and there are not enough tips to help you get better on the OS, as mentioned earlier, just getting on it will enlighten and expose you more. With the aforementioned chapter, tips, guidelines, and help, it is expected that when next you get on this Windows 10, you will perfectly navigate through its features and functions.